D0065305

HOW TO RULE
THE WORLD

HOW TO RULE
THE WORLD

ANDRÉ DE GUILLAUME

CONTENTS

———◆———

About the author

Despite the bitter experience of failing to stage a coup of his own in 1973 (see page 138), André de Guillaume is the embodiment of a dictator in the making. Not only does he display all the characteristics of someone who really wants power, but he would go to extraordinary lengths to get it. Taking inspiration from many of the great leaders through history, de Guillaume encourages readers to believe in their own dreams for reaching the top and offers invaluable advice on how to get there.

How to use this book

This book should be your constant companion on the road to supremacy. Read and digest at leisure; learn the passages by heart and recite them when you feel alone or dispirited; take a pen and write notes in the margins if you have to. Each chapter should be a lesson to you as not all aspects of ruling the world will come as second nature.

Keep a record to chart your progress and to offer reassurance when the finer points of true dictatorship seem forever out of your grasp.

Why Rule the World?

'Those who have been once
intoxicated with power,
and have derived any kind
of emolument from it,
even though but for one year,
can never willingly abandon it.'

EDMUND BURKE

WHY RULE THE WORLD?

POWER HAS A PRETTY POOR IMAGE IN TODAY'S WORLD OF BLEEDING HEARTS AND POLITICAL CORRECTNESS. SOME SAY POWER SHOULD BE SHARED, THAT TOO MUCH POWER IN ONE PERSON'S HANDS IS A BAD THING, AND THAT POWER GOES TO PEOPLE'S HEADS, BUT ONLY PEOPLE *WITHOUT* POWER SAY THESE THINGS, WHILE PEOPLE WHO *HAVE* POWER KNOW THAT NOTHING HAPPENS WITHOUT IT. YOU ARE NOTHING WITHOUT POWER, AND YOUR FORTUNES WILL BLOW WITH THE WIND. WITH POWER YOU ARE A FORCE THAT CAN CHANGE THE WORLD.

Why power is good for you

'Power corrupts. Absolute power is kind of neat.'
– John Lehman

Wielding power does you a world of good. From the moment we are born, we derive the greatest pleasure from having our will obeyed. See how parents come running whenever a child screams for food, attention, a toy (especially another's) or sweets. Children are the greatest dictators – they always get their way. Now imagine the joy if you could command like this throughout your life, the whole world rushing around to placate your inner child. It would be heaven on earth. Not only that, but in addition to peace of mind and a sense that you are a superior person, there are various other spin-off benefits that cannot be ignored:

- riches
- the finest health care money can buy
- classy women
- exquisite material possessions
- international travel

Is it possible to rule the world?

> 'Giving money and power to government is like giving whiskey and car keys to teenage boys.' – P.J. O'Rourke

This book is as much about ruling *your* world, as it is about ruling *the* world. You could go on to create the greatest empire the world has ever known, to subdue all nations under your own colors, and to change the course of history. It is possible. However, do not consider yourself a failure if it doesn't happen quite like this: there are many other ways to lead, dominate, govern, and rule. Playboy founder Hugh Hefner has created an empire of his own, even if it is only inhabited by scantily-clad young women dressed as rabbits. From the boardroom to parliament to the throne room, the lessons in this book will ensure you reach the top in any chosen field and, above all, that you stay there.

The pitfalls and challenges

If it were easy to obtain power, would those who have it protect it as vehemently as they do? No, there are undoubtedly dangers along the way, and you will need all the cunning and perseverance you can muster in order to succeed. Major pitfalls and challenges are outlined in the chapters that follow, where you will learn how to watch your own back while stabbing someone else's, and how to develop the alliances you need to secure a place at the top.

FREDERICK THE GREAT (1712–1786) – MILITARY GENIUS

- The father of Frederick the Great educated his son to become one of the most dominant figures in modern German history.

- He was a cultured man, but Frederick's real genius was for military campaigning.

- He wrote copious military instructions for his generals – on the sustenance of their armies, on the troops' abilities, and on how to set up and secure camp.

- In Prussia, Frederick inherited a well-organized state with an efficient army, which he used to increase the country's status in Europe during the Seven Years' War.

- A despot at heart, he believed that a ruler could carry out his duties efficiently only if he kept control over the government in his own hands.

- He improved his nation's quality of life substantially, introducing economic reforms, granting religious freedom, and abolishing torture.

Why democracy doesn't get things done

Politics has its uses (see *Politics: the fine art of back-stabbing*, page 36), but if you think senators and backbenchers have any real power, think again – this is not a book for those who believe that power resides in parliaments and congresses. Politicians are ruled more by compromise than by their own ambition. They spend endless days dealing with committees and reviews, their hopes and fears dominated by an overwhelming desire to be liked. Democracy is the art of achieving nothing by doing a lot.

True leadership is the exact opposite, and the secret lies in being able to act with absolute conviction. Having real power is being able to say that black is white without fear of contradiction or compromise. This does not make for popular rulers, though, and some will call them despots or dictators, tyrants, or autocrats. This needn't concern you, however, because you will be far too busy to worry about what people say about you – your mind will be set on reaching for the next rung on the ladder.

TEN THINGS DICTATORS CAN DO
THAT CANNOT BE DONE IN A DEMOCRACY

1. Close a television station or newspaper.

2. Refuse to pay the bills.

3. Forget to apply for planning permission.

4. Have their profile on a postage stamp.

5. Change yesterday's weather.

6. Write a guaranteed bestseller.

7. Leave a car double-parked
(although BMW drivers may also do this).

8. Make the trains run on time.

9. Get a taxi after 3AM.

10. Actually change the government.

Why some must lead and others follow

'Being powerful is like being a lady. If you have to tell people you are, you aren't.' – Margaret Thatcher

We learn early in life that not everybody can lead: there is only one head pupil, only one captain of the team. Perhaps you were one of those children who were never put in charge – ignored in the classroom and on the sporting field. You were probably made to think that an ability to lead was only granted to 'naturals.' Well, that was then, and this is now. In a grown-up world, anyone can achieve power if they want it badly enough – it is just a question of knowing how to go about it.

Ask yourself: 'Am I a leader or a follower?' If the idea of amassing great wealth and orchestrating the lives and minds of others appeals to you, read on. You have much to learn.

CHAPTER ONE

Have You Got What it Takes?

—— ◆ ——

'Nature has left this
tincture in the blood,
that all men would be tyrants
if they could.'

DANIEL DEFOE

HAVE YOU GOT WHAT IT TAKES?

THERE IS NO MYSTERY: THIS IS A JOB FOR ONLY THE MOST UNSCRUPULOUS, DRIVEN, AND DETERMINED AMONG US. ASK YOURSELF HOW BADLY YOU WANT TO RULE THE WORLD. IF YOUR WILL IS STRONG ENOUGH, CHANCES ARE YOU CAN MAKE IT. SOME OF US HAVE GREATER RAW MATERIAL WITH WHICH TO WORK THAN OTHERS, AND IT HELPS TO KNOW WHICH QUALITIES YOU SHOULD POSSESS TO START WITH, AND WHICH CAN BE WORKED ON.

The ideal personality of a leader

The following questionnaire will indicate whether you have the right personality to become a great leader.

1. You are quick to settle into a new workplace, reorganizing labor and appointing a network of informers. YES / NO

2. You do your best to complete a task on time, even if you have to break a few heads to get it done. YES / NO

3. You like giving instructions in a loud voice. YES / NO

4. You are always looking for opportunities to undermine your boss's authority. YES / NO

5. You prefer meeting in small conspiratorial groups to interaction with lots of people. YES / NO

6. You find it difficult to suppress a smirk when talking about your feelings. YES / NO

7. After prolonged socializing you feel you need to take from others by force. YES / NO

8. The more people you address at one gathering, the better you feel. YES / NO

9. You are most at ease in a crowd that is chanting your name and saluting you. YES / NO

10. You have Citizen Kane on DVD. YES / NO

HOW DID YOU SCORE?

1–3: give up now.   4–7: borderline, but showing promise.   8–10: you're a natural.

The ideal ruler

'If a prince wants to maintain his rule he must be
prepared not to be virtuous…' – Niccolò Machiavelli

Charisma

Any democratic leader can persuade people to vote for him –
once, at least. But it takes unmistakeable charisma to persuade
men to follow with blind devotion, no matter what.
Unfortunately, you either have it, or you don't. Napoleon had
it, as did Juan Peron and Adolf Hitler. A test for whether or not
you have charisma is to set an acquaintance a series of tasks,
each one more risky than the last. For example, ask them to
lend you money, then to borrow money to give to you, then to
steal money for you. If they keep going each time, you can
safely conclude that you have charisma. If not, you need to find
a better class of friend.

Paranoia

Paranoia in an ordinary citizen is a disease of the mind best
treated with medication. In a leader, however, it is a sign that
you are mentally healthy – everyone *is* after you, after all, just as
you are after *them*. (See *Paranoia: the despot's friend*, page 73.)
Therefore, if you trust no-one, have a propensity for cruelty,
and a blinding self-confidence, you start the race several yards
ahead of your competitors.

Unscrupulousness

A great leader sees what must be done and does it regardless of any consequences to his reputation. Take the Holy Roman Emperor, Charlemagne. He was considered to be a reasonably peaceful man for his time, yet was capable of ordering the execution of 4,500 revolting Saxons as an example to others at Verden in 782AD. The secret here is not to worry about what is wrong or right, only what is *effective*. It may be that all you need is a little subterfuge, deceit, and dissemblance. Unscrupulousness can be nurtured, and you may find it useful to take counsel from Machiavelli, who wrote: 'because men are wretched creatures who would not keep their word to you, you need not keep your word to them.'

Determination

This, too, can be cultivated. Remember that glory and power are rewards to those who strive ever onward, without counting the cost. Hannibal's crossing of the Alps is a good example of this. Although considered one of the great acts of military genius, it was also an act of single-minded determination. He did not care how many elephants or men died along the way, but focussed on his goal of reaching the plains of Italy at whatever price. On achieving any goal, every sacrifice will seem justified, so do not fear to make them. 'Greater love hath no man than this, to lay down his friends for his life,' British Liberal Party leader Jeremy Thorpe once observed in the 1970s. Hannibal understood this.

ATTILA THE HUN (406–53) – LORD OF TERROR

- He ordered that Hun babies have their cheeks slashed to learn to bear pain at an early age.

- He created a network of informants along the Danube to enable him always to have the strategic advantage.

- A great self-publicist, he created his own fear-inspiring image making sure to wreak maximum carnage whenever possible.

- He had his brother Blader murdered in his sleep to consolidate his hold on absolute power.

- He ran the first protection racket, extracting money from the Romans against the threat of violence.

- A polygamist with many mistresses, he died from a hemorrhage on his wedding night to yet another young wife.

What would you do?

What kind of leader would you make? Have you got what it takes to reach the top? How would you react to these following three testing scenarios? (Answers on page 23.)

Scenario one: a troublesome friend

You came to power with the support of a lifelong friend and his influential father. However, your friend is now objecting to some of the things that you do. He is undermining your authority, yet you know you cannot sanction him without incurring the wrath of his father.

Do you:

a) Have a heart-to-heart with him, in the hope that you can work things out between you.

b) Visit the father and ask for his help in achieving a reconciliation between you and your friend.

c) Accuse your friend of plotting against you and have him tortured, until he confesses, then killed. Meanwhile, despatch a trusted friend of the father's to deliver a sealed death warrant to him, to be acted upon while the two of them are joyously greeting each other.

Scenario two: an imminent invasion

You are a fledgling leader of a small kingdom. Having fought most of your life to control the domain, power is now yours. However, a foreign army three times the size of yours is bearing down on you. If you are defeated, you can expect exile, death even. You have one ace up your sleeve – 20,000 prisoners captured in previous battles.

Do you:
a) Try to negotiate terms for peace, using the prisoners as collateral.
b) Use the prisoners to create some kind of distraction while you try to escape to another country.
c) Impale all 20,000 prisoners as a deterrent to the advancing enemy.

Scenario three: a chilling dilemma

You have invaded another country at the head of a mighty army. However, the weather is on the change and it is starting to get a bit cold – freezing, in fact. Your loyal men, who have followed you through thick and thin, are hungry and cold, and must surely start dying in droves unless you decide to call a retreat soon.

Do you:

a) Call a retreat as soon as your men start to suffer, thus preserving your army to fight another day.
b) Sue for peace with the enemy and negotiate food and shelter for your army.
c) Catch the first carriage back home and leave your entire army to be shot, starve, and/or freeze to death.

Working with what you have got

'Fortune is a woman and if she is to be submissive it is necessary to beat and coerce her.' – Niccolò Machiavelli

Not everyone starts off with fully-formed despotic tendencies. Politicians are made by spin doctors and fawning toadies, but true leaders make themselves. Consider the writings of the great leaders, learn their histories and model your behaviour on theirs. Read the business pages and subscribe to *The Economist*. Aim to take one step towards your goal every day: work on your charisma, start a pub brawl, practice saluting in the mirror.

CHAPTER TWO

Apprenticeship: the Wilderness Years

'One man who has a
mind and knows it,
can always beat ten men
who haven't and don't.'

GEORGE BERNARD SHAW

APPRENTICESHIP:
THE WILDERNESS YEARS

ALEXANDER THE GREAT INHERITED THE MACEDONIAN THRONE AT THE AGE OF 20 AND GENGHIS KHAN WAS 22 WHEN ELECTED LEADER OF THE MONOGOLIAN KIYAT. SUCH EARLY ACHIEVERS ARE RARE AND IN MOST CASES A DICTATOR SHOULD EXPECT TO SPEND AT LEAST SOME YEARS IN APPRENTICESHIP. THIS TIME SHOULD BE USED WISELY, DEVELOPING THE SKILLS THAT WILL SERVE WELL WHEN YOUR HOUR OF TRIUMPH COMES AND ESPECIALLY IN ACQUIRING THE CONTACTS AND SHEER PASSION THAT WILL MAKE IT ALL POSSIBLE.

Lowly beginnings:
essential for credibility

'The childhood shows the man,
as morning shows the day.' – John Milton

Even if it is necessary to fabricate the evidence, it is desirable to be deemed of low origin: people are more likely to follow you if they think you share common ground. Hitler was an unemployed 'down-and-out' after leaving the German army in which he was a mere corporal. In the era of high unemployment between two world wars, this made him a man of the people. Napoleon rose from the rank of a junior gunnery officer – a fact he never failed to remind his troops of – while Stalin came from common Georgian peasant stock.

An impoverished background offers plenty of opportunity to experience deprivation and suffering – the roots of most ambition. Attila the Hun understood this when he ordered the slashing of children's cheeks in a bid to toughen them up. Low birth cannot be guaranteed, however, so if you were born with a silver spoon in your mouth, focus on the most miserable aspect of your childhood. Perhaps you were bullied at school, or deprived of something you wanted. Perhaps you spent too little (or too much) time with your parents. Trauma can be found in the most unlikely places, and it is such troubled beginnings that will give you the edge in later life – marking you as different from others – and the edge that will make you a leader.

A constructive childhood

'We have had an Imperial lesson; it may make
us an Empire yet!' – Rudyard Kipling

Leadership qualities should be evident early on. Consider the
tale of baby Hercules, who crushed the serpent that his
stepmother placed in his cradle. Ask your parents for
breakthrough events in your childhood or, if lacking, create a
few for yourself. Be careful here. You want tales of premature
intelligence and wisdom, of unbounded courage, perseverance,
violence or cruelty – *not* stories about how well you mastered
potty training and the day your wore mommy's dress. In the
wrong hands, such examples can lose their context.

A world ruler's education

No education is too good for the would-be despot. Perhaps the
most exclusive was that given to Alexander the Great, who
received one-on-one tuition from the great philosopher, Aristotle.
Many leaders have enjoyed the best education money can buy:
the last Shah of Iran was educated at the exclusive Le Rosey
school, the 'best known private school in Switzerland'. English
Prime Minister Sir Anthony Eden and Prince Paul of Yugoslavia
were classmates – as were many other VIPs – at England's
exclusive Eton, and Madam Chiang Kai-shek was educated at
Wesleyan College, Georgia, in the United States.

- She was bastardised before she was three years old after the annulment of her mother's marriage to Henry VIII in 1536.

- Well educated and fluent in six languages, she inherited intelligence, determination, and shrewdness from both parents.

- When angry she would swear relentlessly and once spat on the clothes of a courtier who had not dressed to her liking.

- She saw the value of being in touch with the people and 'offered her carriage to be taken where the crowd seemed thickest and stood up and thanked the people'.

- She wanted to erect a lasting monument to record '…that this Queen having lived such and such a time, lived and died a virgin.'

- In the last decade of her reign, the standard of living reached the lowest level in the whole of recorded English history.

Ideal hobbies

Hobbies are among the most sophisticated forms of play, usually taken up when children begin to assert themselves as individuals. They can be complex and challenging (building model ships) or brutally simple (snapping the heads off dolls). A future leader should have one of the following or similar pastimes:

Playing at business

This involves a desire to push friends into a structured organization and hold regular board-style meetings. The proceedings, interrupted only by mother bringing in executive refreshments, will run to a strict agenda and will be properly minuted, normally by a younger sister.

An interest in pets

Animals will hold a distinct fascination for young dictators-in-the-making. Favorite activities may involve pulling the wings off moths and butterflies; squashing insects; pouring salt on slugs; and drowning kittens. This indicates an early appreciation of power, as does a preference for dissection in biology class.

Playing with guns

Playing with guns is a natural and healthy pursuit for a youngster. Would-be leaders tend to elaborate on the theme, disarming and detaining their enemies before interrogating them for many hours and returning them, quaking, to their families. Additional hobbies may include shadowing enemies to school at a discreet distance. These children have an acute awareness of psychological warfare and are not likely to be fired on again.

Having pen pals

Here, children may be quick to obtain a PO box from which they take delivery of mysterious packages. Note that their email address is password protected and that they carry a small codebook in their backpack. If they start to develop an interest in cryptic crosswords and old Len Deighton novels, you can be sure there is more to them than meets the eye.

A word on sport

No self-respecting future despot would waste a moment in such a foolish pursuit and for one principal reason: the level playing field. Having to play to a fixed set of rules is bad enough, but why put yourself in a position where you have no starting advantage over your foe?

Networking: making friends for life

It is essential for a leader to demonstrate an ability to dominate others from a very early age. This way you will grow up with a network around you that may offer much support in your adult life. Fortunately all groups of children seek to be dominated by one outstanding child – you just have to make sure it is you.

Here are three invaluable pointers to help you along your way:

- Do not waste time on developing meaningful friendships with people. It is much harder to ask someone you trust to do your dirty work.
- Surround yourself with directionless and malleable toadies. The most useful people in life are often those who are the most useless.
- Those you keep close to you are the people you shouldn't care less about losing.

Emerging from the wilderness

It is time to make yourself known. Continue to build on your network of lackeys and nurture the skills you have acquired so far. You will need to call on both many times as you pursue your destiny to absolute power.

CHAPTER THREE

Career Paths to the Top

'The struggle to the summit itself is
sufficient to fill the heart of man.'

ALBERT CAMUS

CAREER PATHS TO THE TOP

YOUR STRUGGLE TO THE TOP MAY FILL THE HEART, BUT ONLY BEING AT THE TOP WILL FILL THE COFFERS. IN ORDER TO SUCCEED, THEREFORE, IT IS IMPERATIVE THAT YOU CHOOSE A CAREER PATH THAT WILL GUARANTEE YOUR CHANCE OF ATTAINING ABSOLUTE POWER. ONLY THEN CAN YOU FOCUS ON HONING THE SKILLS IN THE PREVIOUS CHAPTER (SEE *THE IDEAL RULER*, PAGE 18), AND BEGIN NETWORKING WITH LIKE-MINDED INDIVIDUALS.

TEN JOBS LIKELY TO LEAD TO WORLD DOMINATION

1. **Salesman:** Where better to master the cloudy relation between truth and reality?

2. **Secretary of a political party:** Stalin and Brezhnev were well rewarded for keeping the minutes.

3. **Film director:** Movie production has long been a satisfying refuge for the megalomaniac.

4. **Computer programmer:** The careers of Bill Gates, Bill Hewlett, and Dave Packard prove that the geek really can inherit the earth.

5. **Soldier:** (See *Military: an officer and a despot*, page 39).

6. **Chef:** Democracy is not an option in a commercial kitchen.

7. **Political advisor:** He who has the ear of the leader may soon have his liver. Former dictator of Zaire, Mobutu Sese Seko, was once the trusted army chief-of-staff to Prime Minister Patrice Lumumba. Needless to say, Lumumba did not last long with such a chief-of-staff.

8. **Parking inspector:** Where a fine-tuned killer instinct is a prerequisite.

9. **Accountant:** Once you have reduced all human flesh and blood to digits on a spreadsheet, it is only a small step to press 'delete.'

10. **Interior decorator:** Albert Speer, Hitler's architect, in fact did some very tasteful interior decorating.

Politics: the fine art of back-stabbing

'Politics is not a science…but an art.'
– Otto von Bismarck

For those seeking to obtain and exercise power, a political career is the ultimate training ground. Many thoughts and actions that are considered utterly unacceptable in civilized society are permitted without qualification in the realm of politics. As Jesse Unruh, speaker of the Californian Assembly, once said: 'if you can't drink a lobbyist's whiskey, take his money, sleep with his women, and still vote against him in the morning, you don't belong in politics.'

A political life is at once dynamic, cut-throat, passionate, and clandestine – a life where opposing sides believe they each have the exclusive monopoly on good sense and that an opponent's views are not only erroneous, but downright dangerous. Any act is therefore justified if it protects society from the excesses of your opponents. It is not uncommon for members of the same political party to oppose each other – that is the beauty of politics. As such, they will do anything they can to bring about another's demise, even though they are supposed to be on the same side. In theory nobody gets hurt. Angry words are exchanged, cold shoulders are given, that is all. Not so in Turkey, however where Turkish MP Fevzi Sihanlioglu met his demise during a violent brawl with a member of Turkey's National Action Party in the Turkish parliament in 2000.

Business: money talks

'Can we change the world? No, but hell we can all try.'
– Rupert Murdoch

Bill Gates, the world's richest man and chairman of Microsoft, didn't have to work. Born into a wealthy family, he inherited millions as a young man and could have spent his entire life as a happy wastrel. Similarly, media mogul Rupert Murdoch could have been content just to play with the *Adelaide News*, left to him by his father in the 1950s.

So what makes these people build such an empire? The answer is sheer power: the ability to have presidents or prime ministers take your call; the thrill of controlling the lives of vast numbers of people, and of seeing your decisions shape entire economies, influencing the very development of society. Murdoch's newspapers can make or break governments, while Gates' technology is almost ubiquitous. All moguls know that it is not money that matters – it's what you do with it. After all, you can't take it with you.

Religion: the velvet hammer

'The more I study religions the more I am convinced
that man never worshipped anything but himself.'
– Sir Richard Francis Burton

We are, perhaps, used to seeing religious leaders as apolitical,
but many great leaders in history are of religious origin. During
the renaissance, for example, popes found themselves fronting
empires. And with a doctrine such as papal infallibility to work
with, this should come as no surprise. Who dares stand against
you when God is on your side? Whilst recent popes have
constrained themselves to ecclesiastical matters, Julius II, the
16th-century 'warrior pope,' rode at the head of a great army.

More recently, following the demise of the Shah in 1979,
the Ayatollah Khomeini of Iran ruled the country as a
theocracy. And the Taliban clerics of Afghanistan proved only
too happy to take up the reins of power. In 2000, Australia
appointed an Anglican archbishop as its effective head of state.
Let's hope that archbishops have come a long way since Henry
II of England had Thomas Beckett put to the sword in
Canterbury Cathedral for meddling in the affairs of state.

Military: an officer and a despot

'Political power grows out of the barrel of a gun.'
– Mao Tse-tung

Of all the professions designed for autocracy, a career in the military is your best bet. There is no mystery why this is so: having an army at your disposal encourages people to take your opinions seriously. A gun at someone's head can focus their thinking. (Such a career path is also beneficial in democracies – the United States was successfully ruled by General Dwight D. Eisenhower between 1952 and 1961 and, in recent years, war hero General Colin Powell has risen to within a bullet or two of the White House.)

Expect to double your chances if you are a war hero. Mustapha Kemal's rule of Turkey was made possible by his being the only Turkish general not to experience a defeat during the First World War. A khaki-clad Margaret Thatcher held her post in 1982 on the back of Britain's victory in the Falklands War, whilst Mao's part in defeating the Japanese effectively delivered him China on a plate in the 1940s. From the time Julius Caesar entered Rome in triumph with his captives in chains behind him, military men have known the truth of the dictum: 'to the victor, the spoils.' And amongst those spoils is power.

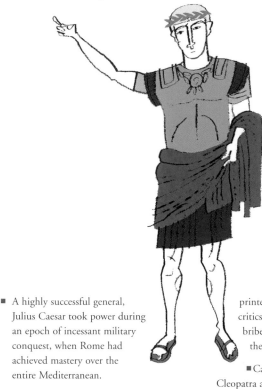

- A highly successful general, Julius Caesar took power during an epoch of incessant military conquest, when Rome had achieved mastery over the entire Mediterranean.

- He presided over the last years of the Roman Republic and broke down its established political procedures to pursue his dictatorial ambitions.

- An excellent administrator, he famously reorganized the calendar from 10 months a year to twelve. July is named after him.

- Soon, Caesar's name became synonymous with absolute power. He had coins printed with his image and his critics lamented his shameless bribery and manipulation of the Roman populace.

- Caesar became infatuated with Cleopatra and was instrumental in her becoming sole ruler in Egypt. They had a son together, Caesarion.

- He was assassinated on the Ides of March 44BC by a group of republican conspirators but his nephew, Octavio, succeeded in taking power and by 32BC, had implemented Rome's first imperial dynasty.

How to get promoted

Ingratiating yourself to your leader and undermining your rivals will ensure that yours is the name on the boss's lips when a vacant position becomes available. Before accepting ask yourself if the job in question will bring you closer to power? Do not deceive yourself: the amount of power you wield is the sole measure of whether a job is worth accepting.

Military coups have much to tell us about where the real power lies. More often than not military dictators are low-ranking officers rather than the senior officers one might expect. This is because senior positions in most armies are rewards for long service and carry little real power. In reality, the power lies with those that are the hub of communications, those that organize and control budgets, those that are gatekeepers between the generals and their troops.

What to do if you are not promoted

If you are passed over for promotion, you may well feel a sense of injury and injustice, anger, frustration, and betrayal. What was rightfully yours has been kept from you, your true value has been denied. Remember these feelings: treasure them. Nurture your grudge. Even the greatest leaders – Churchill and Nixon among them – have been passed over for promotion and it only serves to make them stronger. Let the petty mortals mock and ignore you, for one day you will have your revenge…

How to ensure you get noticed

'Nothing succeeds like the appearance of success.'
– Christopher Lasch

The easiest way to get noticed is either to have a spectacular failure or a spectacular success. The former can be terminal to your career, so you should concentrate on the latter.

The easiest way to be seen as successful is to pass someone else's hard work off as your own, be it their invention, their business, or their intellectual property. This is easy if you are already rich: you can simply buy them out. If money is a problem, there are other methods: get yourself appointed to a project that is nearing completion – a great sporting event such as the Olympics, for instance – and bask in glory as everything comes to fruition. Note how politicians always take the credit for good economic news, but always blame their predecessors for bad. So it must be with you.

CHAPTER FOUR

Achieving Power

———•———

'The great questions of the day will not
be settled by speeches and majority
decisions…but by blood and iron.'

OTTO VON BISMARCK

ACHIEVING POWER

IF YOU HAVE COMPLETED THE EARLY STAGES OF PREPARATION SUCCESSFULLY, YOU ARE NOW WELL ON THE WAY TO VICTORY. STAY FOCUSSED. ACHIEVING ABSOLUTE POWER IS WITHIN EASY REACH — YOU SIMPLY HAVE TO DECIDE HOW YOU ARE GOING TO CLINCH IT.

The election

'Democracy substitutes election by the incompetent
many for appointment by the corrupt few.'
– George Bernard Shaw

Like Hitler, Zimbabwe's Robert Mugabe came to power
through the ballot box, and is one of many leaders to have come
to power by popular proclamation. While it may complicate
matters, and delay your masterplan, there is no disgrace in
coming to power in this way.

In fact, going through the democratic process can give your
rule an aura of legitimacy that is essential when starting off,
even if ultimately you end up cutting a few corners. Zimbabwe
was suspended from the British Commonwealth because of
Mugabe's electoral fraud, but he has kept his hold on power by
going through the motions of being a democrat.

The main challenge, of course, is to keep the power once
you have it, and your people are less likely to bother you if they
feel you have a right to be in charge, however spurious that
right really is.

Succession

'The king is dead. Long live the king.' – Anon

Another way of achieving power legitimately is by being anointed as someone's successor. All monarchies rely on this principal to ensure a swift transfer of power every time a ruler dies – there is no time for dissent or discussion if the new monarch starts his or her reign with immediate effect.

Succession is harder if you don't have royal blood to fall back on, although you could always consider declaring yourself a king or emperor as Julius Caesar and Napoleon did. People will find it hard to overthrow you with their heads bowed – they'll be too scared of the axe that might fall.

Murder – taking direct action

The Scottish king Macbeth, so celebrated by Shakespeare, actually did murder a king called Duncan and seize his throne. If a swift rise to power is what you seek, few acts are more effective than a good murder.

While a court of law could never pin the deed upon him, the Roman Emperor Claudius rose to power following the assassination of his predecessor, Emperor Gaius, at the hands of his own palace guards. According to some accounts, Claudius was declared Emperor against his will on the discovery of the dead emperor's body. Whether this is true or not, Claudius was certainly in the right place at the right time to benefit from a spot of back-stabbing.

Murder has a curious way of clearing the decks for action. England's Richard III had to remove a large number of rivals before he could finally call the throne his own. He is credited with the deaths of Henry VI , Henry's son Edward, his brother Clarence, and his nephews Edward and Richard. Given this, it should come as no surprise that he met an untimely death himself – he was the last English king to die in battle, in 1485.

The coup

'The issues are much too important for the
Chilean voters to be left to decide for themselves.'
– Henry Kissinger

A coup is quick, decisive. Ecuador has seen no fewer than four in recent history. Some may deduce from this that such frequency makes Ecuador unstable and therefore a dangerous place to be. For the despot, however, it is exactly this that offers an irresistible opportunity for coup success.

Follow the examples of others if you are not sure how to organise your coup. There are plenty of methods to choose from. Mohammed Suharto came to power in Indonesia on October 1, 1965, but made sure that another military officer – a Colonel Latief – was blamed and jailed for leading the coup before taking power himself.

Other leaders have done well to look abroad for assistance in their coup success. General Humberto de Alencar Castelo Branco, the army chief who took power from President Goulart in Brazil in 1964, made use of his contacts in the CIA, who then spent over $5 million supporting anti-Goulart candidates in elections and destabilising his government. With such friends as these behind him, Branco found it much easier to seize and hold onto power.

Organising your own coup

> 'We are not dictators, rather instruments
> of the will of our people.' – Joseph Goebbels

Power is rarely given to those who deserve it most: it must be taken. However, you only stay in power with support. Therefore, whether you are taking over a corporation or a country, certain factors must be in place before you start:

You must have a backer

If you married wisely, now is the time to pay a visit to your father-in-law. Can you rely on his support during your final push for power? If you are seeking to ascend a throne, look to your nobles: few monarchs in history have ascended a throne without the support of the most powerful nobles. Perhaps the most celebrated was the Earl of Warwick, named the 'Kingmaker,' owing to his record of securing no fewer than three changes to the English throne.

If your aim is to become a dictator, then you should look no further than the CIA – almost completely autonomous following the demise of the KGB. Indeed, there was a period in the 1970s where no South American government, from Peron in Argentina to Pinochet in Chile and Banzer in Bolivia, could be established without their involvement.

Denigrating the enemy

Whoever you are trying to replace, depicting them and what they represent as wrong or evil is a valuable first step and will justify any measure you might take against them.

There are four things that will turn the hearts of the people against your opponents: corruption, cruelty, injustice, and incompetence. Of all these, incompetence is the most unforgivable, as a certain amount of corruption, cruelty, and injustice is to be expected in a government. Any example you can find will serve as a pretext for your coup, and it is not necessary to prove anything – proof is for courts of law, and even then only in a democracy.

Choosing your moment

Whether staging a coup at work or in the presidential palace, be sure to plan for the start of a weekend. Any politician will tell you that Friday is the ideal day to release bad news, if only because no journalist will follow up the story until Monday. Who knows what may have happened by then? This is the time Argentina chose to invade the Falkland Islands in 1982, the time General Pinochet took over Chile in 1973, and the time Iraq invaded Kuwait in 1990. It should not come as a surprise to learn, therefore, that September 1, 1939 – the day on which Hitler invaded Poland and started the Second World War – was a Friday. By the time they read about it in Monday's papers, it was all over.

If at first you don't succeed

It is possible that you will not succeed the first time. Don't give up: your time will come. The Scottish king Robert the Bruce was roundly defeated in 1306, only to bounce back and reclaim his kingdom at the Battle of Bannockburn in 1314.

Fidel Castro was imprisoned and exiled in the 1950s before finally overthrowing Batista in 1959. Even Dracula eventually reclaimed his Walachian throne after losing it just two months into power. All these men understood the importance of perserverance, and so should you.

LENIN (1870–1924) – RED REVOLUTIONARY

- Lenin's coup of 1917 installed a Bolshevik dictatorship, in Communist guise, and signalled the end of the old Russian Empire.

- The Russian civil war (1918-22) provided the pretext for suspending all existing institutions and wiping out all opposition.

- The Tsar and his family were murdered on Lenin's orders and 'class enemies' were shot by the Chekka (forerunner of the KGB) for 'counter-revolutionary sabotage'.

- The creation of the so-called Soviet Union in 1922 was in reality a brutal reconquest by Lenin's Red Army of the emerging national republics.

- In Lenin's hands, the cinema became an instrument of propaganda. He transferred the film industry to the People's Commissariat for Education under the control of the political police.

- Hundreds of statues of Lenin were erected throughout the Soviet Union and were only pulled down after the collapse of the USSR in 1991.

Revolution

There is a great misconception about revolutions: namely that they result from the activity of the masses. Yet if this were true, the Russians would have contented themselves with the February 1917 revolution – which saw the resignation of the Tsar and the start of a fledgling democracy – rather than plump for the October one, which was altogether more disruptive and bloody. No, the masses watch football games and line up for bread: they do not start revolutions.

So, who does start revolutions and how can you get involved? For starters, the one cardinal rule is to get other people to do the work. Do not, under any circumstances, throw Molotov cocktails or carry banners yourself – you could easily get hurt. Take example from Lenin, the Ayatollah Khomeini, and Yasser Arafat – all exceptional organisers, and only setting foot on home turf once the battle had been won.

Likewise William of Orange, the figurehead of England's Glorious Revolution of 1688, who had to be invited to invade from Holland and arrived to find his predecessor James II already in chains, and a thankful parliament offering him the English crown.

Influence

'If you give me six lines written by the most honest man,
I will find something in them to hang him.'
– Cardinal Richelieu

Sometimes it is not necessary to have the ruling title in order to wield real power, and history is littered with powerbrokers who cleverly manipulated matters behind the scenes, while remaining out of the public eye for the most part.

Such a figure was the infamous Cardinal Richelieu, who became prime minister of France in 1624. He established France as a European power and was responsible for severe repression of the Huguenots. He was the most powerful man in Europe during his lifetime, but everything he did was seemingly under the authority of King Louis XIII.

Another whose power rested largely in an ability to influence those he served was the priest Rasputin. Ingratiating himself to the Imperial Russian family, he soon came to exercise influence over appointments and other royal decisions. His critics, especially amongst the clergy, would mysteriously disappear, or find themselves in exile. Eventually, of course, Rasputin's luck ran out and he was murdered – a victim of his own success.

How you know
when you finally have power

Check the following to see whether or not you really are in control. You should be able to tick off at least seven out of ten.

- People use your 'power name' without having to be reminded (see *Making a name for yourself*, page 85).

- You know tomorrow's headlines before the newspaper editors do.

- Mail from the United Nations is addressed to you and not your predecessor.

- You don't bump into people you don't like anymore.

- Your checks never bounce.

- People laugh at your jokes.

- Someone catches your falling napkin/pen/hat before it hits the floor.

- You get the best seats at sporting events.

- You stop carrying ID.

- Your food taster is always ill.

Enjoying the moment

It's time to pause. This is the moment you have worked long and hard for. How does it feel? Concerned you may have hurt a few people on the way up? Worried your friends and family aren't talking to you? Uncomfortable with blood on your hands?

Of course not. Power is everything you ever dreamed it would be. So enjoy, for tomorrow you must run a country...

CHAPTER FIVE

How to Run a Country

———◆———

'Too bad the only people who
know how to run a country are
driving cabs and cutting hair.'

GEORGE BURNS

HOW TO RUN A COUNTRY

SO YOU HAVE ACHIEVED YOUR ULTIMATE DREAM – YOU ARE RUNNING THE COUNTRY. DO NOT LOSE MOMENTUM AT THIS CRUCIAL TIME, BUT ESTABLISH YOURSELF FIRMLY AS YOUR COUNTRY'S LEADER, BOTH DOMESTICALLY AND INTERNATIONALLY. A GOOD WAY OF MAKING SURE THIS HAPPENS IS BY SEVERING AS MANY CONNECTIONS AS POSSIBLE WITH THE WAY THINGS WERE BEFORE YOU CAME TO POWER. SUCCESS IS GUARANTEED IF THE FOLLOWING MEASURES ARE TAKEN THE INSTANT YOU ARE IN POWER.

Change the names of major cities

A subtle yet effective way of showing the world of commerce that you are in total control. Try to keep things simple, however. Start by choosing your favorite name – it may be your own. Depending on preference simply add one of the following suffixes: -ville, -town/ton, -grad, -ria, or -berg for each new city. Alternatively, use the same name each time: according to the ancient historian Plutarch, Alexander the Great was responsible for founding no fewer than 70 Alexandrias.

Change the national flag

Nothing heralds a new regime quicker than a change of flag. Avoid argument by designing the flag yourself. You can take one of several approaches:

- Choose your favorite color – say, salmon pink
- Choose your favorite flora or fauna – a fish
- Choose your country's main export – a bicycle

If you cannot decide which to go for, simply combine two or more of the above. By starting mass production immediately, thereby creating employment opportunities, you are unlikely to meet with resistance.

Change the name of the country

A time-honored authoritarian tactic that has the added advantage of raising revenue, if only by boosting international sales of your country's stamps (see *Ten things dictators can do that cannot be done in a democracy*, page 13). Placing 'Democratic Republic of…' or 'People's Republic of…' in front of your country's existing name may prove sufficient if inspiration is lacking. However, try to avoid 'Dictatorship of…' or 'Police State of…' as they can give the wrong impression.

If you're feeling really bold, try changing the name of the country to something quite different altogether. This can have a wonderfully disorienting effect on your friends and foes alike – wrong-footing those with a strong sense of national identity and confusing the perception of your international profile. A good example of how this can be effective is with the former Union of Soviet Socialist Republics. Now known as the Confederation of Independent States, this has the ring of a much friendlier club to join. Or take Zimbabwe, formerly Rhodesia, where the determination to establish independence from British colonialism cannot be denied. Incidentally Rhodesia itself is a fine example of applying one's own name with pride.

Acting the part

Adopt the characteristics of a leader

If you are going to be in the public eye, you must portray the right image – surprisingly simple if you follow these tips:

- Insist on having every whim obeyed, no matter how quirky. Nero made his horse a Consul of Rome. If you can get away with that, then people will almost certainly fall into line on bigger issues.

- Start quoting philosophers and historic figures. ('I'm sure Churchill would have agreed…,' 'That is a question that I, and Plato before me, have spent much time considering…').

- Adopt a tone of infinite wisdom by ending every sentence with a question.

- Above all, gesticulate. Wave your hands about when you give speeches.

Dress like a leader

Get your tailor to run up a uniform without delay. Perhaps you are a member of the military already, in which case your standard dress uniform would probably do, but there's no need to be restricted to this. Express yourself. Give in to that fancy for a bit of brocade, for sporting medals and epaulettes, or for wearing knee-high riding boots. Tartan trim from a Scottish regiment? Turned-up shoes from the Greeks, a turban from the Bengal Lancers, a tunic from the Vatican Guard? Use your imagination – you are now an international figure, after all.

Remember. Nothing inspires respect quite like a military uniform – it carries with it an unmistakeable subliminal message of power. Hitler and Stalin knew this, Idi Amin, Mussolini, Franco, the list goes on.

Milking the media

Fidel Castro, the world's longest-reigning living leader, never loses an opportunity to tell the people of Cuba what he wants and how he wants it, and neither should you. Treat your subjects to regular television and radio broadcasts. Fidel is famous for his long speeches and, in May 1959, he addressed a grateful nation on television for six hours. You too could be such an inspiration.

Using the media to avoid criticism

Handled badly, the media can be as great a threat to you as your worst enemy. In time, you will learn to use the media to your advantage – it is a question of knowing how to manipulate with it. Television cameras should always shoot you from below to accentuate your height, and shoot your opponents from above, to make them seem puny. In the hands of the right editor, any video footage can be altered to your advantage.

One great tactic is the 'snow' news story. If something negative about you is about to hit the media, release something more sensational. You can scan the headlines to see how this ploy is used time and time again.

Feathering the nest

With absolute rule comes the obligation to have the very best facilities at your disposal. Anything less is an insult to your people. Aspire to the likes of King Hassan II of Morocco, who has seven palaces, 250 horses, countless camels, ostriches, and zebras and at least 1,000 cattle.

Use this checklist as a guide to the essentials that you should aim for within the first 100 days of power:

- One large and ostentatious palace. Space to roam is important: Haile Selassie, Ethiopia's 'Lion of Judah,' allowed real lions to roam about his Jubilee Palace.
- At least one smaller country retreat (consider Hitler's mountain retreat at Berchtesgaden).
- Two private jets (one for parts).
- Three bulletproof Rolls Royces (you can't just have one and, once you have two, you might as well have three).
- One large yacht (if you find yourself running a landlocked country, you may choose to keep your yacht moored where there is sea, say in the Caribbean).
- A kitchen staffed by the finest chefs.
- A food taster.
- A large number of servants.

Building your bureaucracy

You will need a considerable army of bureaucrats to staff the bloated organs of your new state, so now is the time to find those sinecures for your friends and family. Not only will this offer employment and rapid advancement to droves of opportunistic individuals but, entirely dependent on your favors, they will always be ready to do your bidding. Provided you keep various departments in direct competition with each other, internal rivalries will dilute any threat to your supreme power.

Remember to employ only plodding administrators, however, those lacking any real talent. Lenin underestimated Stalin's ambition when he made him General Secretary of the Bolshevik party. When Lenin succumbed to illness and subsequently suffered a stroke in 1922, Stalin took charge. Lenin belatedly realised what a threat Stalin was and wrote a secret letter advising the Congress to have him removed. But Stalin delayed the Congress and suppressed the letter. Such are the quirks of fate: if Lenin's stroke had not left him paralysed, perhaps Stalin would today only occupy a footnote in the history books.

Settling old scores

> 'When he seizes a state, the new ruler must determine all
> the injuries he will need to inflict. He must inflict them
> once and for all.' – Niccolò Machiavelli

Most people will have a handful of enemies and, while it is a
pipe dream for most people to actually get rid of them, for you
this is a reality. First, identify your possible foes:

- Who did you push aside to get to the top?
- Who was influential, but didn't help you enough?
- Are there any friends/supporters of the previous ruler?
- Who has an unhealthy interest in the status quo?
- Has anyone been rude or disrespectful to you?
- Who knows too much about your past?

Now, think what you would like to do to them.

- Assassination: Be creative here, England's King Edward IV
  had the Duke of Clarence drowned in 'Malmsey wine.'
- Public Execution: From burning heretics such as Thomas
  Cranmer, to decapitating the likes of Marie Antoinette.
- Imprisonment: A remote parched island prison has been
  popular in the past. Napoleon was exiled twice by the allied
  nations of Europe.
- Torture: The mainstay of the Spanish Inquisition in
  the 16th century, used to persecute heretics in the
  Catholic Church.

- Following in his father's footsteps, MacArthur lived his entire life in the United States Army, and learned at an early age that a MacArthur is always in charge.

- MacArthur is largely credited with single-handedly selling the American people on the Selective Service Act of 1917, even though the United States government was resisting entry into the war.

- With a flamboyant style, matched by feats of courage on the battlefield, MacArthur became the most decorated American soldier of the First World War.

- After the war, MacArthur was appointed Superintendent of the U.S. Military Academy at West Point, and dragged the institution into the 20th century.

- MacArthur's single-minded drive and resourcefulness rolled back the Japanese presence in the Philippines during the Second World War, bringing about their surrender on board the U.S.S. Missouri in 1945.

- MacArthur fought publicly over military tactics with the Truman administration during the Korean War and was relieved of his command when he wanted to continue the war with China.

Lawmaking

> 'If anyone buys from the son or the slave of
> another man, without witnesses or a contract…,
> or if he take it in charge, he is considered a thief
> and shall be put to death.' – The Code of Hammurabi

Since the Code of Hammurabi, created back in around 1780BC, great leaders have also been great lawmakers. The process is slow and inefficient in a democracy, where legislation may need considerable debate before being passed into law, only to be open to re-interpretation at a later date. This is not a problem for modern-day despots, however, who can quite literally take the law into their own hands. A good way to start is by compiling your own legal dictionary. For example:

- **Defamation:** Absolutely anything bad said about you.
- **Judiciary**: A group of paid admirers who validate your laws.
- **Jury**: A group of paid admirers who are there to overrule any judge who forgets who's paying his salary.
- **Law**: The way you want things to be, expressed in writing or verbally. There can never be any confusion in a dictatorship about how a law is to be interpreted – as the person who made it up, you are there to clarify matters at any time.
- **Lawyer**: Someone who advises on the best way of concealing offshore investments.
- **Congress**: A group of paid admirers who agree to all your edicts and applaud you frequently in front of television cameras.

Decision-making

Few decisions are ever made in a democracy: someone has a bright idea, it is drafted, a committee sits, an enquiry is held, a commission is established, reports are tabled, recommendations are considered, questions asked, memorandums issued. Just as something is about to happen, a new government gets elected and the idea is buried.

In a dictatorship, all-powerful rule centers on making things happen. In coming to any decision, therefore, there are just two things to consider:

- Will my decision confound my enemies?
- Will my decision make me richer?

Take as an example, whether to enforce driving on the left or right. By changing the side of the road on which people drive, not only would you cause consternation and inconvenience your enemies, but it is likely to mean many revenue-raising possibilities – higher insurance premiums, overseas investment in road works and signage, higher taxes to pay for it all.

A word on posterity

For history to remember you with any degree of affection, it is essential that you do at least one thing well (see also *Posterity: leaving your mark*, page 117). Find an aspect of social reform to champion, make better communications your mission, become a patron of the arts. Mussolini was a cruel, vain and unpleasant despot, but what people remember about his regime was that he made the trains of Italy run on time. Germany has Hitler to thank for its autobahns, and most of us are still using the Gregorian calendar established by Pope Gregory XIII in 1582.

CHAPTER SIX

Staying in Power

'...a perpetual and restless
desire of power after power,
that ceaseth only in death.'

THOMAS HOBBES

STAYING IN POWER

ACHIEVING POWER IS SOMETHING YOU SHOULD BE PROUD OF. YOU DO NOT WANT TO END UP LIKE ENGLAND'S EDWARD V, WHO REIGNED FOR ALL OF TWO MONTHS BEFORE HE WAS DEPOSED. POWER IS BEST ENJOYED OVER A LONG PERIOD OF TIME, SO YOUR FIRST DUTY IS TO KEEP YOUR OPPONENTS AT BAY IN ORDER TO ENJOY YOUR NEW POSITION.

Paranoia: the despot's friend

'Whoever is responsible for another's becoming powerful ruins himself, because this power is brought into being either by ingenuity or by force, and both of these are suspect to the one who has become powerful.'
– Niccolò Machiavelli

Do not delude yourself that, once in power, you are safe. Now is the time to face the one great truth – that everybody is out to get you. Your food could be poisoned, your guards could be assassins, and your confidantes are almost certainly spies. An awareness that your life – or, more importantly, your power – could be taken from you at any time can offer protection. You must be eternally vigilant and trust nobody. Above all, avoid the likes of Raymond Mercader who asked Leon Trotsky to look at an article he was writing and turned out to have an icepick concealed about his person.

You might think that such a situation would cause sleepless nights. For weak leaders, perhaps, but not for the strong. Although everyone must seem suspicious to you, they also present a challenge to your professionalism. You will use every skill in seeking the truth and take great pleasure in exposing those who are not what they claim to be.

How to tell who is plotting against you

It is safest to assume that everyone is plotting against you. As you cannot deal with everyone, concentrate on those people who present the greatest threat:

Your supporters: The first group of people to watch are those who helped you to power. All your accomplices are now your rivals. Keep them close to you and they will have little room to maneuver.

Your predecessor(s): Whoever you replace at the top will undoubtedly want the glory back at any price. Even if you allow them to live, you should confine them. Under no circumstances allow them to go into exile. Like boomerangs, they have a habit of coming back.

The enemies of your sponsors: If you have been bankrolled into power, you can be sure that your sponsor has enemies who will see your success as your sponsor's success.

Your family: Napoleon Bonaparte had the right idea by finding jobs for many of his relatives. He made his older brother, Joseph, King of Naples, and found work for most of his other siblings.

Great plots from history

> 'A man cannot be too careful in the choice
> of his enemies.' – Oscar Wilde

There are few things more satisfying than a good plot. Fortunately, for every plot that succeeds, there are dozens that fail. Sometimes even the best plots don't quite work: either there is a fatal flaw in the plan or an individual proves unreliable.

Assassination of Abraham Lincoln, 1865

Like all good plots, this was delightfully simple. There were three targets – Lincoln, Vice-president Andrew Johnson, and Secretary of State William Seward. The three were to be assassinated simultaneously in three different locations, thus destabilising the government. The nine or so conspirators, headed by actor John Wilkes Booth, hoped thereby to allow the southern states of America, recently defeated in the American Civil War, to rise up again. The plot was only partially successful. Lincoln was killed, but Seward survived his stab wound and George Atzerodt, the man assigned to kill Johnson, chickened out and got drunk instead.

Moral: In order to avoid a fate like Lincoln's, avoid second rate dramas.

The Gunpowder Plot, 1604

As much as a year in the planning, this breathtaking plot – to blow up the British Parliament on the day it was to be opened by protestant King James I – was masterminded by dissident catholic Robert Catesby and the mercenary Guy or 'Guido' Fawkes. Amazingly, Fawkes was able to lease a cellar underneath Parliament and, between March 1604 and the legendary November 5 (another Friday, incidentally, see *Choosing your moment*, page 50), filled it with gunpowder. Before the appointed day, however, one of the plotters started dropping none-too-subtle hints to friends. Not surprisingly, news filtered back to the authorities and Fawkes *et al* were apprehended.

Moral: Do not lease your cellar to known mercenary soldiers for them to store things in.

The Recchioni Plot, 1931

Soho Shopkeeper Emidio Recchioni tried to have Mussolini assassinated. In 1931, he gave money to an anarchist called Angelo Sbardellotto, who bought two bombs and a revolver and headed for Rome. Unfortunately, Sbardellotto wasn't a very good assassin. After several attempts, he was apprehended and forced to confess. Italy demanded Recchioni's extradition, but the British government refused to hand him over.

Moral: Mussolini would have done well to note the company Recchioni kept. One of his customers in London's Soho was avowed anti-fascist George Orwell.

FIDEL CASTRO (b.1927) – EL CAUDILLO

- The son of a self-made plantation owner, Castro persuaded his parents to send him to school at the age of six.

- On New Year's Day 1959, his determination to remove Batista from power paid off after three previous attempts.

- He made an enemy of the United States when he turned to Communist Russia for support and allowed the Russians to establish long-range ballistic missles on Cuba.

- A man of the people, Castro took property owned by non-Cubans, and collectivized agriculture to the benefit of the laborers.

- Despite a number of attempts to knock him from his post, Castro has now been in power for a record 44 years.

- Despite abject poverty in Cuba owing to the collapse of the Soviet Union, Castro's subjects continue to reward him with their loyalty.

Maintaining control

'I'm glad I'm not Brezhnev. Being the Russian leader in
the Kremlin, you never know if someone's tape-recording
what you say.' – Richard Nixon

Inside your borders

One group has been omitted from all talk of plots and
insurrection so far – the masses. As in the case of the 1991 Soviet
coup in Russia and at the fall of the Berlin Wall, the general
public can represent a thorny problem, if roused. Fortunately, it
does not take much to keep them quiet and, in order to prevent
an uprising, it is necessary to prove that oppression is merely an
illusion. If the people are being well-fed (Hitler promised
Germany 'bread and freedom') and entertained (as with the sight
of Christians being eaten by lions), what reason would they have
to struggle to their feet and take to the streets? It would seem
that modern tactics revolve around sport and television. In fact
sport *on* television is unrivalled for success.

Outside your borders

The 19th-century phrase 'the Great Game' was coined to
describe the clandestine diplomatic, economic, and political
shenanigans conducted by major European powers of the time –
Britain, Russia, France, and Germany – in pursuit of their plans

for global dominance. During this period, revolutions were started, regimes toppled, leaders assassinated, puppet kings appointed, guns were run, and spies abounded – all in the name of the national interest. It continues today – only now it is called globalization. If you wish to rule the world, then you too must play 'the Great Game.' Spread yourself across the world, open bank accounts abroad, and post employees to key centers of economic and political influence. Wherever you can, put local thugs on your payroll.

Cruel and unusual punishments

Of course, even with bread and circuses, you will occasionally have to apprehend and punish dissidents. It's your duty to do so, and to do so publicly. Guy Fawkes (see *The gunpowder plot*, page 76) was hung, drawn, and quartered – a gruesome practice specially reserved for those convicted of treason. It involves being hanged until barely conscious, before having the stomach slit open and innards burned. Finally the head is removed and the body chopped in four – quite literally 'quartered.' Ivan the Terrible of Russia was wholesale in his punishments. In one week, he had the 60,000 inhabitants of Novgorod slaughtered – some were drowned, others impaled or flogged to death, some even roasted alive. If the power you wield is in a corporation, local government regulation may prevent you from using these tactics. Don't let that prevent you from reminding those under you of the achievements of men such as Ivan, however.

Playing favorites

One final note about staying in power. As Napoleon once said, a man will fight harder for his interests than for his rights. The main way to keep people on your side is to reward them for doing so. If someone struggles night and day to meet your every whim, let them have a desk a little closer to yours, preferably at the expense of someone who is keeping their head down. It will send everyone the right signal: 'please the boss and you'll be treated well.' Dog trainers call it positive reinforcement. You'll find people are a little easier to train.

CHAPTER SEVEN

Advanced World Rule

———◆———

'Power tends to corrupt and absolute
power corrupts absolutely.'

LORD ACTON

ADVANCED WORLD RULE

AN ABSOLUTE RULER MAY WELL STRIDE ABOUT IN AN IMPRESSIVE UNIFORM, LIVE A LIFE OF WANTON EXTRAVAGANCE AND BE DRIVEN BY CRIPPLING PARANOIA – THIS WE KNOW. BUT THE TRUE DESPOT WILL DEVIATE FROM SUCH ESTABLISHED NORMS. IN DELIGHTFUL, ECCENTRIC FASHION, A REALLY MASTERFUL RULER WILL ASTOUND US WITH THE VERY IRRATIONALITY OF HIS EXCESSES.

Founding a faith

> 'In England there are sixty different religious sects, and
> only one sauce.' – the Marquis Domenico Caracciolo

You have already established yourself as a 'brand.' Your image is
everywhere and you are in control. How do you ensure that
your influence endures? Even beyond death?

The natural progression for many great rulers – from
Alexander the Great to the warrior-philosopher Mohamed
through Ras Tafari in more recent times – has been to start a
religion. Think of the benefits:

- It is an activity that involves conformity on a huge scale,
  with a strict adherence to one dominant point of view.

- It offers infinite revenue-raising opportunities.

- A country cannot have too many religions.

- If you get it right, you may even go global.

- The tax implications are impressive.

Reinvent yourself

Earlier chapters have shown how many leaders came to power with names other than those with which they were born (see *Making a name for yourself*, page 85) – nothing impresses the masses more than an air of mystique. The significance of this is even greater when founding a religion, as Ras Tafari Makonnen proved by taking on the name Haile Selassie ('Might of the Trinity'). By adopting a more spiritual identity you can change how your people see you – they will perceive your rule as transcending the 'here and now.'

Get published

For the benefit of your followers, it is important to have your key beliefs written down. Without *Mein Kampf*, Hitler would exist for us today only in old newsreels; without Kim Il-Sung's memoir, *With the Century*, we would know even less about North Korea's late communist dictator. Not all books by great leaders – Margaret Thatcher's *The Downing Street Years*, for example – lead to the establishment of a religion or cult. But without one, you and your religion are in trouble. Without your words of wisdom to guide them, your followers will turn inevitably to someone else (see *Essential reading for world leaders*, page 123).

Making a name for yourself

Over the years, many great tyrants and actors have seen the value of improving on their name, and there are several ways of doing this:

- Take on a sobriquet or nickname. How much more fearsome did Ivan Vasiljevich become, for example, having added 'the Terrible' to his name. Many others (Catherine, Alfred, Alexander, Peter) achieved their place in history by adding 'the Great.' And consider the effect of Vlad Dracula, otherwise known as Vlad the Impaler.

- Assume a 'power name.' Choose something appropriate to your position, or a particular characteristic. Leadership has always proved popular, for example, and there are various alternatives; Hitler and Mussolini opted for the straight translation in Der Führer and Il Duce.

- Be creative. Think carefully about the image you wish to convey. Stalin translates as Man of Steel, Atatürk as Father of the Turks.

Propaganda: the despot's friend

'A truth that's told with bad intent
Beats all the lies you can invent,' – William Blake

Propaganda is a most exciting tool. Remember that truth is relative. A fact need only be as true as you want it to be. A great propagandist is able to make the most shameful lies seem credible and the most blatant truths implausible. You will discover that, as George Orwell suggested in his novel *Nineteen Eighty-four*, two plus two really can equal five.

Control of the media is paramount

It may be necessary to buy up troublesome media outlets. Follow Russian premier Vladimir Putin's example. He had a court rule that the dissident television station NTV was in fact owned by the state's gas company, Gazprom. As soon as the court ruling was passed, Gazprom stepped in, sacked all the station's dissident management and established a Putin-friendly team of its own.

If a buyout isn't feasible, simply close the media outlet down. You barely need to find a pretext – Indonesia's President Suharto didn't when he closed down mass-circulation magazine *Tempo* following its innocuous story about his government's purchase of navy ships.

Media relations 101

Of course, it is unlikely that you will be able to control every media outlet so here are a number of cardinal rules for you to follow when, inevitably, your paths cross.

- Assume a humorous, avuncular manner. A superficial charm can conceal a multitude of sins.

- Blame your problems on the previous ruling power. Note how Zimbabwe's President Mugabe has continued to blame Britain for the plight of his country, even though it pulled out of Zimbabwe over 25 years ago.

- Never confess to being a dictator. Simply say the time is not right for democratic elections. Indeed, the time is never right unless you are absolutely certain of winning.

- Invite the journalist to see things from your viewpoint. This renders criticism virtually impossible.

Events, rallies, and parades

A small point, but, alongside the spreading of misinformation, another great tactic is the big event. Everyone enjoys a good show: brass bands, flag-waving, smart uniforms, and unbounded patriotism.

- He established himself as a ruthless ruler of the People's Republic of China by taking over three million dissenters prisoner, executing many and brainwashing others.

- Against all odds, Mao defeated Chiang Kai-shek's far superior army by adapting the techniques of guerrilla warfare from the writings of ancient military experts.

- He understood that peasants were the key to revolution and appealed to their sense of injustice at the hands of their landlords.

- With his Agrarian Reform Law, he literally exterminated the landowning classes and handed the land to the peasants.

- Mao will be remembered as a socialist, a poet, a military strategist and ruthless ruler – one of the world's most powerful rulers ever.

- Mao was supreme at developing the 'cult of personality'. Twenty years after his death, he is still worshipped as a demi-god, and saviour of the Chinese people.

The big idea

Every ambitious ruler has a big idea – from Genghis Khan to George Bush Jr. – and it invariably involves world domination. Unable to contain themselves within the borders of their own countries, Napoleon, Stalin, Attila the Hun, Julius Caesar, and others all took it upon themselves to export their lifestyle and culture in a forthright manner.

Great rulers and their big ideas

QUOTE	NAME
'This country should be under one God (Allah).'	Ayatollah Khomeini
'This country should be under one God, and God should be under me.'	Henry VIII
'Everyone's got to be a Christian – now.'	Emperor Constantine
'In five years' time, we'll be self-sufficient in food.'	Joseph Stalin
'No-one's allowed to wear a fez.'	Mustapha Kemal
'I should rule the world.'	Genghis Khan
'Everyone I don't like should die.'	Vlad the Impaler

Your big idea

All successful totalitarian rulers have a big idea. Only the nature of the vision varies. It could be the Aryan paradise of the Nazis or the classless stage of communism as preached by the Marxist-Leninists. The main purpose of the big idea is to justify all the brutalities and sacrifices of your regime and ensure the loyalty of your followers.

You may feel that your people should speak a different language, or that entire sections of the population should move to another part of the country – away from a newly discovered gold mine, for example – or that a particular mountain is in the wrong place. Whatever it is: think big. You are all-powerful and can do whatever you want.

How to start a war

People often take exception to a despot's big idea – particularly when it involves ruling other parts of the world. Inevitably you will find yourself at war.

The right way to go about it

- Be prepared: As a self-respecting dictator, you will no doubt have at your disposal large numbers of well-trained, fanatically loyal troops. Make sure you also have access to overseas aid – preferably from a known superpower.

- Surprise your enemy: As soon as you are ready, attack. Avoid the diplomacy that usually precedes a war between democracies – written letters, despatched envoys, parliamentary debates – unless they are delaying tactics and allow you to prepare your troops. As Hitler discovered when he invaded Holland and Belgium, and Bonnie Prince Charlie discovered at the battle of Preston Pans, it is much easier to defeat someone when they're putting on the cocoa and preparing for bed.

The wrong way to go about it

- Never actually declare war: Give no notice, no warning and, under no circumstances, say you are in a state of war. War is a legal term and, once at war, there are troublesome rules that countries are obliged to follow. The Geneva Convention is a valuable point of reference on this matter.

War? What war?

If you don't actually declare war, you can call it whatever you like. Popular euphemisms include: 'incident,' 'conflict,' 'insurgence,' 'uprising,' 'police action,' 'incursion,' 'border incident,' 'problem,' 'affair,' 'minor military exchange,' 'skirmish,' and 'security breach.' None of these will trouble your own population unduly. Neither will they alert your enemy to your true intention – to make what is his, yours.

Building your empire

'How is the Empire?' – George V *(last words)*

Once you start building a power base for yourself, you will find it very difficult to stop. Your first conquest will simply give you a taste for more. Napoleon, Hitler, and Alexander the Great knew this only too well – as soon as one campaign was over, they were thinking of their next. You should too, for a ruler that stays still is a ruler ripe for the taking.

Imagine you had £100 to buy some clothes. You would probably buy a few essential items – some shoes, and maybe a shirt. But what if you had £100,000 to spend? Just imagine the fashion crimes, colour explosions, and 'wear once and throw away' items you might buy. Building an empire works along the same lines. When you have everything that you need, or can reasonably want, what is left? The answer is: you don't care, as long as it belongs to you.

A word of warning, however. To paraphrase Edward Gibbons' immortal work *The Decline and Fall of the Roman Empire*, they all come to an end eventually. So don't be disappointed if your own empire is short-lived. Grab what you can when you can, and never lose a hold on your original power base – you may need to seek refuge there some day.

SIX GREAT EMPIRES

- **Roman Empire** *3rd century BC to 4th century AD*
  At its peak, this empire stretched as far north as Scotland and as far south as Egypt.

- **Han Empire** *2nd century BC to 2nd century AD*
  Established the shape of modern China and oversaw the invention of paper.

- **Ottoman Empire** *16th to 19th century*
  Administrated from Istanbul, this was the largest and most influential of the Muslim empires.

- **British Empire** *17th to 20th century*
  Largely trade-driven enterprise whose lasting contributions to the world will be soccer, cricket, and afternoon tea.

- **News Corporation** *1950s to present day*
  Rupert Murdoch's ever-expanding media empire.

- **Bertelsmann** *21st century*
  The German conglomerate owns no companies in sub-Saharan Africa, Turkey, or Uzbekistan. But that's about it.

A word about failure

There is no such thing as failure. You may experience setbacks, but you cannot lose: win your war and you can start pillaging straight away; lose, and a flood of foreign aid will comfort you in your defeat. Either way, your personal success is assured.

CHAPTER EIGHT

Power and Wealth

———•———

'Money was never a big motivation for me,
except as a way to keep score.
The real excitement is playing the game.'

DONALD TRUMP

POWER AND WEALTH

MONEY AND POWER GO HAND IN HAND. IF YOU HAVE CASH, THEN POWER WILL SURELY FOLLOW. IF YOU HAVE POWER, THEN OPPORTUNITIES TO ACHIEVE GREAT WEALTH ARE EVERYWHERE. ONE THING IS CERTAIN: IF YOU HAVE NEITHER, YOU'RE NOT GOING ANYWHERE.

Wealth: a natural consequence of power

'I believe that the power to make money is a
gift from God.' – John D. Rockefeller

There is no point having power if you don't intend to use it.
Why have a gun if you're not prepared to fire it, or a Porsche if
you cannot drive? Yes, you could use your power to feed the
hungry or clothe the naked, but there are plenty of people
doing that already. Having money broadens your horizons and
will always buy you a refuge should you fall from grace.

Henry Ford changed the world with his wealth. Corporate
guru Lee Iacocca claims that America would not have had a
middle class without him. At the peak of his personal power,
before the Great Depression of the 1930s, Ford ruled over
100,000 employees, a shipping fleet, a railway, several mines,
and thousands of hectares of plantations like a true dictator,
having little time for democracy.

Inspiration may also come from the developing world, where
you will find the best examples of leaders amassing fortunes when
no-one else is looking. Ferdinand Marcos reportedly fled the
Philippines with carry-on luggage containing $8.9 million in
jewellery, cash and bonds, for example, and had stashed as much
as $13 billion in Swiss bank accounts prior to his demise.

Legitimate wealth creation

'If you can count your money, you don't have a
billion dollars.' – J. Paul Getty

It is wise to use the term 'legitimate' or 'lawful' here rather than
words such as 'honest' or 'good.' Just because something is right
in the eyes of the law, does not mean that it is particularly
decent or respectable. Besides, when you are in a position of
power, it is up to you to decide exactly what legitimate means
(see *Lawmaking*, page 68). None of the following activities are
particularly morally good, but as long as they are lawful, you
need lose no sleep making money from them.

1. Raping the mineral wealth from a third world country
   without paying compensation. (You will need a contract.)
2. Taking possession of someone else's art treasures or gold
   bullion as 'reparations,' though you must first defeat them
   in a war.
3. Running a casino.
4. Owning a tobacco plantation.
5. Supplying arms.
6. Dumping toxic or nuclear waste.
7. Mowing down virgin rainforest.

Protecting your financial interests

An invitation to the annual Bilderberg meeting is a valid indication of your status in the world. You will join over a hundred of the most powerful people on the planet – bankers, captains of industry, and leading politicians – to discuss the interests of international capitalism, free from the restraints of democratic processes, media reportage, minutes and agendas. What do they talk about at these three-day summits? They do not say. What do they decide? Nobody knows. Members of the press who attend are sworn to secrecy. Everything said is 'off the record,' but it seems to be a sure fire way of making sure your financial interests are secure. This is an elitist get together and competition for attendance is high. To guarantee entry, consider adopting one of the following titles:

- Chief Adviser to…
- Commissioner
- Senator
- Chairman
- Founding Partner
- President (in the company sense)
- Minister of
- Associate
- Member, House of Lords
- Director (not in the film sense)

Money and sex: a warning

While the subject of power and love is dealt with in the next chapter (see page 105), it does not seem appropriate to discuss the issue of money without mentioning the opposite sex. Be warned that, from the moment you acquire your money, the opposite sex will find you irresistible, and will offer to satisfy your every need in return for the chance to help you spend that fortune. They will try to seduce you, they will throw themselves at your feet and they will generally debase themselves. There is only one stance to take on this issue: *Let it happen.*

Did anyone pity oil tycoon J. Howard Marshall II, the 89-year-old billionaire who married 26-year-old Anna Nicole Smith? He only survived 14 months of marriage, but he died with a smile on his face. Ms Smith earned $450 million from his estate for her trouble. What did Marshall care? He was long gone by the time the matter was resolved in court.

AL CAPONE (1899–1947) – SCARFACE

- The golden rule for Capone was to keep outwardly respectable, no matter what clandestine activity was going on behind closed doors.

- Even as he was running Chicago brothels and speakeasys, he was telling his neighbors he dealt in secondhand furniture.

- Capone went on to build a big business, employing thousands of truck drivers, prostitutes, accountants, petty crooks, musicians, bartenders. He even had a few politicians on the payroll.

- Displaying violent tendencies at an early age, he was expelled from school at fourteen for hitting a teacher.

- He epitomized the concept of loyalty by shooting a man for calling his friend a dago pimp for refusing to lend him money.

- When he was finally sent to jail for racketeering and tax evasion, he managed to smuggle several thousands of dollars in with him in the handle of a tennis racquet and was able to live in luxury.

Financial planning for despots

'Make money by fair means if you can; if not, by any
means so long as you make money.' – Horace

Having amassed your wealth, you will inevitably spend a good
deal of it on life's little incidentals – the payroll for your cronies,
money for bribes, and the maintenance of various wives,
mistresses, and palaces. However, you should have some left
over – you are doing something wrong if you haven't – and it is
best to find a safe and remote place in which to keep it.

By far the best option is to set up an International Business
Company (IBC) in a tax haven. Like any other company, an
IBC conducts all its business with the outside world but, unlike
any other business, it being based in a tax haven excludes it
from paying any tax. There are countries that will bend over
backwards to attract IBCs, and they will guarantee absolute
secrecy and confidentiality by law. Moreover, by a stroke of
good fortune most tax havens are in highly desirable tropical
locations, making them ideal holiday destinations.

FIVE GREAT TAX HAVENS

1. **Belize** Formerly British Honduras, Belize is a sub-tropical Caribbean paradise just south of Mexico. It has become a favorite tax haven owing to its International Business Companies Act, which makes leaving your money here a very attractive proposition.

2. **Switzerland** A favorite of Ferdinand Marcos, it is estimated that over 30% of the world's 'protected' private wealth resides here. While some Swiss banks have bowed to international pressure and will now disclose information about their investors in extreme circumstances, most are thankfully quite happy to take your money and stay mum.

3. **Bermuda** The 62,000 occupants of the 360 islands known as Bermuda enjoy one of the highest standards of living in the world, thanks to a sympathetic 'asset-protection' regime that has operated since the islands' heyday in the 1960s and 1970s.

4. **The Seychelles** A group of 100 islands in the Indian Ocean, the Seychelles is a nice place to visit and an even nicer place to keep cash – IBCs are tax-free for the first 20 years.

5. **Commonwealth of Dominica** If time is an issue, Dominica is one of the most straightforward, no questions asked, of all tax havens. And it's all 100% legal.

Keeping your money clean

As Al Capone ably demonstrated, you can get away with murder if only you wear clean spats and give generously to charity. The latter is a good way of laundering money, particularly if the charity in question is one of your own. 'Going legit' (or at least going through the motions of appearing to be so) has been the goal of many criminals. By some accounts, more than half the $530 million set up in 'charity funds' by President Suharto was paid out to his cronies rather than Indonesia's needy poor.

Money earned from prostitution or drug running can be cleaned up in no time if put through a tax haven (see *Five great tax havens*, page 103), used to buy stocks and shares, or put into charitable trusts.

CHAPTER NINE

Power and Love

'Power is the ultimate aphrodisiac.'

HENRY KISSINGER

POWER AND LOVE

WHETHER IT IS DOWN TO THE UNIFORM OR THE LURE OF UNFETTERED AMBITION, THERE IS NO DENYING THAT A POWERFUL MAN IS NEVER SHORT OF ADMIRERS. IT RARELY HAS ANYTHING TO DO WITH LOOKS, AND EVEN THE MOST ABHORRENT OF PEOPLE CAN ATTRACT THE OPPOSITE SEX MERELY BY FLASHING A LITTLE CASH. WHY THIS SHOULD BE IS A MYSTERY, BUT BE IN NO DOUBT THAT IT IS A PHENOMENON YOU CAN USE TO YOUR ADVANTAGE.

Marriage

'Caesar's wife must be above suspicion.' – Julius Caesar

You may require many women to cater to your needs – the Sassanid king Chosroes II had a harem of 3,000 wives as well as 12,000 female slaves – but a leader has only one consort. This is a political appointment, not an emotional one, so it is important that you get it right. Choose wrongly and the results can be messy: Henry VIII of England found himself having to chop and change wives several times.

Marriage is excellent for cementing alliances between yourself and another ruler or financier. Once you have decided on the alliance that most benefits you, you should choose the type of consort best suited to your personality (see *Dating tips for dictators*, page 108).

Do your homework

Marrying someone like Lucrezia Borgia could get a man into trouble. Married the first time at age 13, her father, Pope Alexander VI, had her divorced once he found a better alliance to pursue. Lucrezia's brother Caesar had her second husband strangled when he also outlived any political advantage. Her third husband took an enormous dowry before agreeing to marry her, and managed to outlive her.

Dating tips for dictators

'If women didn't exist, all the money in the world would have no meaning.' – Aristotle Onassis

Although it is imperative that any alliance should be made to your greatest benefit, you should not rule out personality, since this too has its advantages.

The blank slate: Just two things are known about Eva Braun – that she was Hitler's mistress, and that she committed suicide with him. If she had an opinion about anything, we don't know. If your preference is total domination, therefore, a 'blank slate' is what you need.

The entertainer: The ideal choice if your rule needs a glimmer of glamour. Where would Juan Peron have been without Evita? Take great care with her as a very passionate entertainer may well contribute to your downfall.

The Lady Macbeth: Just occasionally you may find a true soul mate in your ascension to greatness – someone willing to dedicate herself to your cause. Even better if she is brighter, quicker and less scrupulous than you as was the case of the wife of Chiang Kai-Shek. The only person he could truly trust, she was his minister for aviation during the war against the Japanese in the 1930s and later helped him found the Republic of Taiwan.

NAPOLEON BONAPARTE (1769–1821) – EMPIRE BUILDER

- A great lover of women, Napoleon was married twice and had several mistresses.

- He was a military genius, and seemed unstoppable as his power within Europe stretched ever wider, with many of his siblings ruling regions beneath him.

- During his reign, Napoleon made some very formidable enemies, not least Alexander I of Russia, Frederick William III of Prussia, George III of England and Francis I of Austria.

- He understood that the fate of the French Empire lay in more hands than just his own and was careful to surround himself with many reliable and loyal marshals.

- Even having been exiled once to Elba, Napoleon did not relinquish power readily and returned to fight another day.

- He was able to captivate the hearts of his people despite the great hardship that his imperial campaigns caused.

Great power-partnerships

Some people need another person to complete them – on their own they are modest achievers, but in harness they can take on the world. Just occasionally such people come together and sparks fly. The results can be memorable.

Louis XVI and Marie Antoinette: Louis of France and Marie Antoinette of Austria were literally made for each other. They were raised expecting to marry each other, and so they did.

Napoleon and Josephine: Jospehine Beauharnais was the ultimate entertainer and an ideal companion – as Napoleon himself said: 'I win battles, Josephine wins hearts.' While they were married for 13 years, Napoleon eventually realised that Josephine was never going to give him the heir he sought and therefore, very practically, had their marriage annulled. Although she was the only woman he ever loved, he realised that power had to come first.

Bill and Hillary Clinton: Hillary is a classic 'Lady Macbeth' (see *Dating tips for dictators*, page 108). She allies herself to her husband's career, while openly displaying ambitions of her own. One can only speculate as to the reason why this relationship has lasted as long as it has.

Not-so-great power partnerships

Despite the most promising beginnings, it is possible for an alliance to degenerate over time. Under no circumstances should such a relationship be endured. You need to be ruthless here, and let a partner go the moment they cease to be of use.

Anthony and Cleopatra: Mark Anthony and Octavius shared control of the entire Roman republic following the assassination of Julius Caesar. The alliance was strengthened by Anthony's marriage to Octavius's sister (Octavia). But, like a fool, Anthony allowed love to color his judgement and he left Octavia and Rome for Cleopatra and Egypt. Naturally, this damaged Anthony's relationship with Octavius and it was not long before the ruling partners were at war. Octavius defeated Anthony and Cleopatra at the Battle of Actium and then pursued them into Alexandria where they both committed suicide in 30BC.

Nelson and Winnie Mandela: It all started so well. Winnie was true to Nelson, campaigning on his behalf during his incarceration in various South African jails. But once they were reunited, Nelson saw her for the electoral liability she was and sent her packing. No matter how loyal and tenacious she had been in support of his freedom, her Lady-Macbeth instincts had got the better of Winnie and she had made too many of the wrong kind of friends. Nelson was unyielding – the woman had to go.

Mistresses

There is no limit to the number of mistresses you can have, as long as you provide your wife with an heir and try to maintain at least a little discretion.

Aspire to the likes of England's King Charles II, who sired at least 14 illegitimate children by several mistresses, and had dalliances with many more. The most famous, and most loyal to him, was the actress Nell Gwyn, who bore him two children and set up a 'home-from-home' for him. He is reputed to have asked on his deathbed that she be provided for. More recently, Philippine President Joseph Estrada – a former screen actor – has developed a wandering eye. In addition to his loyal wife, he reputedly has at least five mistresses, three of whom have borne him children.

Premier perks

The US presidency is one of the most powerful jobs in the world. While the activities of President Bill Clinton are a matter of public record, it is worth noting that such historical pillars as Presidents James A. Garfield, Warren G. Harding, Franklin D. Roosevelt, Dwight D. Eisenhower, and Lyndon B. Johnson all had mistresses. Perhaps the most celebrated presidential mistress was Marilyn Monroe whose relationship with John F. Kennedy in the 1960s remains one of ambiguity to this day.

US presidents don't have the monopoly on mistresses though. Greek prime minister Andreas Papandreou once famously arrived back from open-heart surgery in London with a former airline hostess on his arm. He subsequently divorced his wife and declared his mistress First Lady of Greece.

Mars and Venus in the throne room

'Wives are young men's mistresses, companions for
middle age, and old men's nurses.' – Francis Bacon

Leaders are different to the people they lead, and so can play a
different game. Here are a few well-chosen tips for dictators.

1. **Always go to sleep mid-argument**. This will give your
   mistress the opportunity to dwell on the folly of disagreeing
   with you and allows her to wake nice and early the next
   morning with a heartfelt apology.
2. **Never give something with one hand that you can't take
   back with the other**. Most despots like to shower their
   mistresses with gifts and jewels. This is fine provided the
   material can be recovered at short notice – by paid
   thugs if necessary.
3. **Love for the masses means never having to say you're
   sorry**; for the powerful it means never having to apply
   one's self to housework.
4. **Always keep at least one mistress who can cook**. Others
   may be prettier or smarter, but nothing beats a good winter
   broth or a crème brulée.
5. **Fidelity is for cowards**.

The supreme sacrifice: celibacy

'If I am to disclose to you what I should prefer if I follow
the inclination of my nature, it is this: beggar-woman
and single, far rather than queen and married!'
– Elizabeth I

Elizabeth I decided not to marry her childhood sweetheart
Robert Dudley and stayed married to her throne instead. This
was particularly useful when tinkering with the delicate
balance of power in Europe. It meant Elizabeth was always
available to discuss marital alliances with the other crowned
heads of Europe, even if she never actually got around to
agreeing to any of them.

It doesn't always work

All things considered, celibacy can cause more problems than it
solves. Edward the Confessor of England died in 1051 without
an heir. The fight that followed his death led to the invasion of
England by claimant William of Normandy in 1066. But for
Edward's desire to be left alone, the world would be a very
different place today.

A word about polygamy

'Man is a natural polygamist. He always has one
woman leading him by the nose and another hanging on
to his coat-tails.' – Henry Louis Mencken

Polygamy is illegal in most Western societies. You can have as
many lovers as you want, but remember: you can only marry
one of them at a time. However, Islamic law allows for a man to
take up to four wives provided he can provide for each of them
properly. Not surprisingly, therefore, multiple wives are a sign of
a rich and powerful man in many Muslim countries.

CHAPTER TEN

Posterity: Leaving Your Mark

'The main thing is to make
history, not to write it.'

OTTO VON BISMARCK

POSTERITY:
LEAVING YOUR MARK

MATERIAL WEALTH AND UNFETTERED POWER MAY SEEM LIKE ENDS IN THEMSELVES, BUT NO TRUE LEADER SEEKS POWER SOLELY FOR HIMSELF. LEADERS ARE VISIONARIES, WITH THEIR EYES ON THE FUTURE. THEY WANT TO SHAPE THE WORLD, RATHER THAN BE SHAPED BY IT. THEY WANT TO LEAVE THEIR MARK.

Public buildings and monuments

Many of history's great despots shared a love for a particular kind of architecture. The buildings of ancient Rome, fascist Germany, and Moscow have much in common: big blocks of stone, large square portals, wide streets and squares, imposing vistas – all built to last. You, too, can make your mark in this area.

To succeed in this discipline, consider the following essential elements:

- **Scale**: Proportions should be designed for giants. Portals should be wide and ceilings high. Any stairs should be a struggle to climb. The subliminal message should be clear and effective – we are big, so don't mess with us. (When forced to retreat from the Boas River, Alexander the Great ordered a huge camp to be built, with tents and beds made for eight-foot-tall warriors. Any warring tribe from the east, he mooted, would seriously consider pitching battle.)

- **Statues**: No public space is complete without heroic statues. You may wish to represent warriors from your country's noble past. Or perhaps, you could commission some sculptures of yourself – a bust for the lobby, and some full-length statues for the courtyard, mounted on a steed, even. A good sculpture is very hard to destroy, as the Russians discovered when they tried to smash all the statues of Lenin in the early 1990s.

- **Focus**: In contrast to religious buildings, whose spires and domes reach up to the heavens, your building should look down on the city surrounding it. It should be imposing, leaving your people with a daunting sense of their own insignificance. A large empty square in front of the building will improve the overall effect.

- **No public exit**: People may enter your building of their own free will or by invitation, but they will leave at your pleasure. The message to the masses should be: don't bother me unless you have to – you may not make it home tonight.

- **Balcony**: The Kremlin in Moscow is the ideal public building. Not only does it look impenetrable and foreboding, but it has a great platform for viewing parades. The parapet on a balcony should be at chest height. This way you can duck rotten fruit and bullets, but will still be able to wave at your people without the need to have your trousers pressed first.

Your eccentricities

In addition to public works, you would do well to develop the odd eccentricity in order to distract people from what you are really up to. Newsreel footage of Mussolini shows him to have been a pompous ass, swaggering and pouting at 1930s fascist rallies. Elect, yourself, to wear a funny hat, grow an amusing moustache, or wear enormous pairs of trousers. Like the conjuror that distracts his audience at the crucial moment, a good leader knows the sort of attention he wants and where he wants it.

Memoirs: the quest for credibility

'History will be kind to me, for I intend to write it.'
— Sir Winston Churchill

Otto von Bismarck may have preferred making history to writing it, but he still spent his last years working on his memoirs. Unless you have a really reliable and sycophantic biographer, as Samuel Johnson did with Boswell, it is probably best if you write your own diary. It's a time-honoured way for leaders to set the record straight and to settle a few old scores at the same time. Some leaders, like Ferdinand Marcos left it too late. His memoirs remained unfinished on his death in 1989, and he left nobody literate enough to complete them. Therefore, you are advised to write early and write often. You never know when you might be called to account for your life.

TEN GREAT MEMOIRS:
ESSENTIAL READING FOR WORLD LEADERS

1. *El Día Decisivo, 11 de Septiembre de 1973* by Augusto Pinochet Ugarte. Pinochet modestly demonstrates his brilliant generalship and a deep patriotic concern for his country as he describes how he saved Chile from its democratically-elected government.

2. *Mein Kampf* by Adolf Hitler. 'My struggle.' If only he had mastered painting of the human figure.

3. *Memoir: The Singapore Story* by Lee Kuan Yew. After discussions with my publisher, I have decided I'd rather sell my book in the Singapore market than say something that might get me sued by the litigious Mr Lee.

4. *Memoirs* by Otto Von Bismarck. Unsinkable!

5. *Memoirs of the Second World War* (6 volumes) by Winston Churchill. Reputedly written with significant assistance from a large office of staff, this is a highly personal account of Churchill's 'finest hour.'

6. *My Rise and Fall* by Benito Mussolini. Two volumes: the first published in 1928, the second completed in the months before his assassination in April 1945 and published in 1948.

7. *RN: The Memoirs of Richard Nixon* by Richard Nixon. Transcribed from tapes, perhaps, this short volume contains everything RN could remember.

8. *The Downing Street Years* by Margaret Thatcher. The 'Iron Lady' plays down her many achievements.

9. *With the Century* by Kim Il Sung. The 'eternal leader' of North Korea tells of his humble beginnings and the struggle against capitalism.

10. *How to Rule the World* by André de Guillaume. If you read only one of the books from the list, make it this one.

Children: becoming a patriarch

Given your undoubted virility, and your skilfully-chosen marital alliance (see *Marriage*, page 107), it is only a matter of time before you produce a legitimate heir. Children are, of course, a burden in your youth and a comfort in your dotage. The trick is to place the burden on someone else, while saving the comfort for yourself.

You are breeding a new leader for the world, not a whining, dependent weakling, and there are a few steps to take to make sure you produce a successor to be proud of. (Remember: legitimate succession is the only succession you need worry about.)

1. Place the newborn into the care of a seasoned professional – mothers, though no doubt well-intentioned, are just amateurs when it comes to child-rearing.
2. Put them down for a good school. An exclusive British public school is ideal. (See *A world ruler's education*, page 28). Above all your child must grow up to the loneliness of command – it will be very hard for them to oppress someone they went to school with.
3. Teach skills that will stand a child in good stead in later life. Encourage them to start a share portfolio with their pocket money, and develop an interest in activities such as hunting and shooting.

BARONESS THATCHER (b.1925) - THE IRON LADY

- At the age of ten, Margaret displayed great oratorical skills, winning a prize at the Grantham Eisteddfod for reciting poetry.

- In 1945 she became the Treasurer of Oxford University Conservative Association.

- From early on Margaret was engaged in politics, recalling in 1995 'I was always a "true blue"… I never doubted where my political loyalties lay.'

- She was confident in her own abilities: 'I don't believe in the possibility of defeat. It simply doesn't exist.'

- She was sensitive to media accusations of dictatorial behaviour: 'I drive people but its my job to do that, but it's utterly ridiculous to call me a dictator', 1984.

- Her political beliefs reflected a healthy respect for financial independence: 'No one would remember the Good Samaritan if he'd only had good intentions. He had money as well.'

Things we remember about the dictators… and what they actually did

The first Chinese emperor, Qin Shi Huang, was a brutal and inflexible man. Merely reporting bad news to him was enough to get you executed. He burned the works of Confucius, introduced the death penalty for free thinking, and was universally feared by his people. By digging deep, you can discover these things about the man, yet history records his greatest achievement as the commencement of the Great Wall of China back in 221BC. Alexander the Great was a drunkard and a megalomaniac, and thought he was a god. He put thousands of innocents to the sword. At the same time, he founded an empire and built the city of Alexandria – now one of the wonders of the ancient world – and so history praises him. What these examples show is that men of vision are allowed greater licence to perform acts of enormous barbarity, so long as they create great things as well. You can learn from this. If you're giving your people a hard time, put up an enormous dome or divert a great river: posterity is bound to forgive you your faults (see also *A word on posterity*, page 70).

CHAPTER ELEVEN

On Retirement

———•———

'It is time I stepped aside for a less
experienced and less able man.'

PROFESSOR SCOTT ELLEDGE

ON RETIREMENT

MOST GREAT LEADERS WOULD PREFER TO DIE ON THE JOB. UNFORTUNATELY, THIS IS NOT ALWAYS POSSIBLE. INSTEAD YOU SHOULD AIM FOR A RETIREMENT THAT ALLOWS YOU TO QUIT – LIKE ALL THE BEST CHAMPIONS – WHILE YOU'RE ON TOP, AND WITHOUT LETTING GO OF SOME OF THE PERKS.

Retirement checklist

In civilian life, a retiree will set about obtaining vouchers for cheap travel on public transport and joining the local seniors club. Not so the despot. Here is a list of the key things you should do.

- **Clear the decks:** Make one final purge of all your potential opponents. Mao's 'Cultural Revolution' was such a purge.
- **Find a successor:** The qualities of the right successor(s) are covered below. If there is no obvious replacement for you, follow the example of Lee Kwan Yew in Singapore and pretend to pass your power to a democratically elected assembly. Of course, this assembly will be riddled with your cronies and will be established under a constitution of your own devising.
- **Secure your money:** If you have been saving wisely for your retirement, you should by now have well-laundered funds to support you in your golden years. It's time to move them out of harm's way. (See *Five great tax havens*, page 103.).
- **Find an ideal retirement location:** This should be the best location for both your physical and fiscal health.
- **Select your retirement companions:** Now that your alliances have borne fruit, there is no need to maintain any pretence of being happily married. Choose a companion to occupy you during the long, idle afternoons that lie ahead. Mussolini chose his mistress Clara Petacci, Hitler had Eva Braun.

Choosing your moment

You will know when the time comes. It will happen sometime between finally amassing all the wealth you could possibly desire, and running out of novel and amusing ways of spending it. It will happen when you start turning down invitations to summits, when you stop noticing the deferential salutes, and when you run out of things to say in your weekly television or radio broadcasts. You will simply wake up one morning and realise it's time to find a younger man for the job. When this happens, tell no-one, but set about your retirement in absolute secrecy. The moment someone announces their impending retirement they are a lame duck.

Choosing your successor

Be sure to choose your successor before your successor chooses you. Once word gets out that you are looking to retire, all sorts of furtive and unlikely candidates will start cracking their knuckles and trying on their dress uniforms. Ideally, your successor should be a blood relation – blood is thicker than water and you may not trust a relative, but you will always know where they live. If this is not possible, then you must choose someone whose general skills are inferior to yours. In other words, if you want to be remembered as a great leader, make sure your successor is an idiot.

Second-rate successors

People seldom remember who came after great leaders. Who remembers that John Adams succeeded George Washington, for example. Here are some really bad seconds from history:

Edward II of England (1284-1327): Edward I was a great warrior and visionary, earning himself the title 'Hammer of the Scots.' His son Edward II, however, was a loser. He was defeated by Robert the Bruce at the Battle of Bannockburn, and suffered losses in Ireland too. His barons plotted against him as did his wife, Isabella, who deposed and murdered Edward with the help of her lover, Roger Mortimer.

Perdiccas (c.360-320): Alexander the Great handed control of his empire to his general, Perdiccas, who was to keep the empire running until Alexander's unborn son was old enough to take control. By the time the boy was thirteen, Perdiccas had been murdered by his soldiers and replaced by a rival.

Ogödei Kha'an (c.1200): At the time of his death in 1227, Genghis Khan's empire stretched from Korea in the east to Hungary in the west. His son Ogödei Kha'an then became leader and did... nothing, except oversee its dismantling into three smaller kingdoms. Is the name Ogödei Kha'an familiar to you? Enough said.

How to retire without really letting go

Having worked so hard to acquire power in the first place, you will naturally be reluctant to let it go. Augusto Pinochet and Kim Il Sung both felt the same way. Pinochet changed the Chilean constitution to enable him to remain a senator in the parliament for the rest of his life. No need for elections – just a healthy stipend and the perks of high office for ever after. North Korea's dictator Kim Il Sung had an even better idea. Although he died in 1994, and was succeeded by his son, Kim Jong Il, he decreed himself the country's 'eternal president' – a position that means he still outranks his successor to this day.

How to get away with it all

Ultimately, retirement is about getting away with it all and not having to pay for the various crimes you may have committed during your reign of terror. Fortunately, nature is on your side. The aging process will have made you look less dynamic as you have got older. This is the time to take up a walking stick, put on a slight limp, and use a wheelchair to get on airplanes. You could even wear an oxygen mask from time to time. Chances are people will treat you less as a former despot, and more as a revered elder statesmen, welcome the world over.

The comeback

'Short retirement urges sweet return.' – John Milton

As soon as your successor begins to do things differently – and he will – you may feel an urge to make a comeback. It is human nature. Some can resist such an urge while others – Napoleon, Hannibal, Mussolini, for example – cannot. Napoleon was set on a comeback from the moment he stepped onto the island of Elba. Despite setbacks, Hannibal never missed an opportunity to re-enter the fray against the Romans. And Mussolini, who lost his power in 1943, regrouped in northern Italy and was on the comeback trail within the year. While it is advisable to avoid following these examples, you may find it impossible to resist. But be warned, however. If at first you fail to retire gracefully, you may find yourself a victim of your successor's purge (see *How to tell who is plotting against you*, page 74).

- Despite being a talented artist, Hitler was rejected by the Viennese Academy of Fine Arts.

- From an early age he displayed a pathological hatred of Jews and Marxists, liberalism, and the Hapsburg monarchy.

- He showed great courage serving during the First World War, and was awarded the Iron Cross (First Class) for bravery.

- The first time Hitler attended a meeting at the German Workers' Party (former National Socialist Party) was as an informer on behalf of the Reichswehr.

- A skilled orator, he played on national resentment of the failing economy, presenting himself to the masses as a saviour. The Nazi vote jumped dramatically from 810,000 to 6,409,000 in the 1930 election.

- A nihilist at heart, when Hitler knew he could not survive he vowed Germany, too, should be destroyed.

Dictator demises

We know a surprising amount about the demise of many a despot, and yet there are a few whose fates remain shrouded in mystery. After eight years as dictator of Uganda, the brutal Idi Amin disappeared. Some rumours place him in Saudi Arabia, but who knows for sure? He made good his escape. Or take Adolf Hitler, whose body was allegedly never found by the Russians when they invaded Berlin in 1945. There will always be those of us who believe he is still alive and sunning himself on a beach in Rio de Janeiro.

You don't have to be a military despot to disappear – sometimes ordinary leaders can go too. In 1967 Australian prime minister Harold Holt disappeared while swimming off a beach. His body was never recovered, and this gave root to all sorts of speculation, including a suggestion that he had been picked up by a Russian submarine.

The lesson here is plain: if things are looking bad for you during your time in power, leave early and cover your tracks well. However you choose to do it, make sure your departure is dramatic or mysterious. Then your place in history is assured.

Do not follow the example of British MP John Stonehouse who, having fallen heavily into debt, left a pile of clothes on a Miami beach and fled to Rio with his secretary. After two years, he was captured and returned to the UK to face a jail sentence.

Famous last words

'Don't let it end like this. Tell them I said something.'
– Pancho Villa

So said the Mexican revolutionary to newspaper journalists as he lay dying by an assassin's hand. Given that you, like Pancho Villa, may not be able to predict the exact moment of your departure, it's best to have something prepared in advance. You may wish to try some of these for inspiration:

- 'I do not have to forgive my enemies. I have had them all shot.' – Ramon Maria Narvaez

- 'So, now all is gone – Empire, Body and Soul!' – Henry VIII

- 'I desire to go to Hell and not to Heaven. In the former I shall enjoy the company of popes, kings and princes, while in the latter are only beggars, monks and apostles.' – Niccolò Machiavelli

- 'There are no more other worlds to conquer!' – Alexander the Great

- 'History teaches you that dictators never end up well.' – General Augusto Pinochet

André de Guillaume
– my attempted coup

In 1973, fair stood the wind for despots. The powers that be were throwing cash at anyone who could spell 'anti-Communist' and, if you had a uniform and Aviator sunglasses, here was your chance to run a country.

At the time I was a junior officer in the Cashman Islands militia having studied briefly at the Royal Military College, Sandhurst. The Cashmans are a small archipelago in the Indian Ocean best known for their sympathetic tax laws, and I was truly shocked with what was going on there. The fledgling democratic government, having inherited a business-friendly bureaucracy from our former colonial masters, the French, was making radical and damaging changes to the country. They had built schools, roads and hospitals, instituted programs to care for the sick, elderly, and unemployed, and announced free and open elections would be held on a regular basis.

By the time it was announced that a value-added goods and services tax would be introduced to fund this crazy socialism, I knew something had to be done. Several of us got together with some of the islands' sympathetic French businessmen. One of them gave us a business card of a contact he said had links with a reputable intelligence agency. I wrote immediately and, within weeks, we received an application form for a 'Category B (Island nations)' coup grant. Only six officers were to be privy to the plan. While we had some advantages – such as guns – we realised at an early stage that we would have to plan everything down to the last detail if we were to succeed. Secrecy was essential. To avoid suspicion, we met weekly at a local barbershop in the main island's capital, Port au Lait, under the pretense of forming a barbershop quartet.

Everything was ready. We chose a Friday afternoon for our coup, planning to take out the media outlets on the main island first to control the flow of information, displace the government over the weekend while members of the security forces were at home, and secure the airport to prevent the old regime from fleeing the country. By Monday, the country would be ours, and a more pro-business tax regime could be installed. Following Lenin's example in the October 1917 Russian revolution, I was to set up a center of operations several kilometres away while the military tasks were accomplished and then, after Port au Lait was secured, I would enter the city in triumph and assume leadership of the country.

At 1600hrs, our troops stormed the only radio station in Port au Lait. Back at the center of operations, I tuned in my transistor radio, waiting for the regular broadcasts of music to be replaced with Tommy Steele's rendition of 'Half a Sixpence.' That was to be our signal. At the airport, two of our operatives took up positions in the line at the check-in desk. It would only be a matter of time before they reached the front of the line and the airport was secured. At 1620hrs, the 'glam rock' on the radio ceased abruptly. It was Tommy Steele, but not the song we were expecting. We listened in consternation as two verses of 'If the Rain's Got to Fall' were broadcast. What had gone wrong? Dared we take a chance or should we wait for the right song? Suddenly there was a scratching sound as if a stylus were being dragged across vinyl and an announcer's voice came crackling over the airwaves: 'Sorry: wrong side.' A moment later, Side A was playing and we sprang into action.

By the time our assault team arrived at the government building in the center of Port au Lait, however, things were looking bad. Timing is crucial for any coup and the Tommy Steele mix-up had cost us precious minutes. Being Friday afternoon, everyone had left promptly for the weekend and our men had missed storming the building by a solitary minute.

Of course, back at the center of operations, I did not know any of this. Assuming that everything was going to plan, I ordered my own troops to get into their jeep and make for the prime Minister's residence, where I was to perform the *coup de grace*. As we approached the residence, I recall how my heart swelled. I was just minutes from power, minutes from rescuing the country from its democratic madness. I thought of the decrees I would issue, and the measures I would impose. It wasn't just about cheaper champagne. It was about a lower tax environment across the board, and turning any revenue into presidential cars, boats, planes, and residences.

It was all easier than we could have expected. The door was open when we arrived. The servant who greeted us said that the Prime Minister was in the garden and would be with us shortly, and would we like a drink while we waited? Half an hour later, we were on our second refill and the Prime Minister had yet to appear. I sent one of my men to find out what was going on. Ten minutes later, when he had not returned, I sent another, and then a third and final man.

It was only then that I realised I was alone, and it was getting dark. I reached for the light switch. When the light came on, all I could see were armed policemen, their weapons aimed at my heart. 'Captain de Guillaume, I presume,' said a voice. I turned and there in front of me was the Prime Minister. It had been a trap – but how could they have known? At that moment, the door opened and a familiar face appeared. A wave of realisation swept over me. Of course: the barber.

I was released from Port au Lait prison in 1990 and was deported. I secured a small teaching post at a school in Fort Benning, Georgia, where I was able to give a generation of attentive and zealous Latin American students the benefits of my experience. I lectured mainly on personal grooming, but they often pestered me to relate the story of my own coup attempt, and I have never tired of telling it.

André de Guillaume

WHO'S WHO IN
HOW TO RULE THE WORLD

First published in the United States of America in 2003
by Chicago Review Press, Incorporated
814 North Franklin Street
Chicago, Illinois 60610

Library of Congress Cataloging-in-Publication Data
available from the Library of Congress.

Conceived and produced by
Elwin Street Limited
79 St John Street
London EC1M 4NR
www.elwinstreet.com

Illustrations: Robin Chevalier

ISBN 1-55652-497-8

Printed in Singapore

10 9 8 7 6 5 4 3